Greg Almond, is a specialist claimant personal injury Solicitor. He is Head of Personal Injury at Aticus Law in Manchester, Wilmslow and London. He has specialised in Personal injury throughout his career as a solicitor.

Greg qualified as a solicitor in 2006 and has specialised in Personal Injury for more than 11 years, dealing with high value and niche personal injury claims, often acting for clients who have suffered life changing injuries following serious accidents. Having championed a campaign to highlight the dangers of home hair dye products, Greg met with MPs and posed questions direct to Ministers, resulting in a greater awareness of the potential dangers of some products.

Greg continues to campaign for safer cosmetic treatment procedures and products. As a direct result, Greg has become the Solicitor of choice in the UK for clients who have suffered severe reactions following their use of home hair dye products or other more complicated cosmetic procedures that have gone wrong. He has appeared regularly in the National and local press, including the One Show, BBC news and the Times and is a regular go to commentator on this area of the law.

Greg has extensive experience in working on behalf of both claimants and defendants. Representing clients on a national basis, Greg and his team are always happy to meet clients at their home or at our offices in Manchester, Cheshire or London.

Greg is a Council member of Manchester Law Society and he is a member of the Association of Personal Injury Lawyers.

An Introduction to Beauty Negligence Claims – A Practical Guide for the Personal Injury Practitioner

An Introduction to Beauty Negligence Claims – A Practical Guide for the Personal Injury Practitioner

Greg Almond

LLB (Hons)

Solicitor

Dispute Resolution & Personal Injury

Law Brief Publishing

Published 2019 by Law Brief Publishing, an imprint of Law Brief Publishing Ltd
30 The Parks
Minehead
Somerset
TA24 8BT

www.lawbriefpublishing.com

Paperback: 978-1-911035-89-3

PREFACE

The primary aim of this book is to assist the personal injury practitioner when considering new enquiries and when handling beauty claims – it is an entry level guide.

It will be especially useful for practitioners who have not undertaken this work before and are looking to expand their service offering.

As such, in part one of the book, I will describe common beauty treatments with a brief explanation as to how they should be performed by a competent practitioner. Key practice notes will be provided.

This section will also address the common problems and how to help your client pursue a claim for compensation avoiding the pitfalls.

Part Two is intended to be a practical guide for practitioners and will include a sample client questionnaire and risk assessment checklist. I will also consider patch tests, claims involving children, disclosure and public liability insurance issues. There is also a chapter discussing cosmetic surgery claims.

I hope this guide will assist as a useful resource to personal injury practitioners when dealing with beauty negligence claims.

The law quoted is believed to be accurate on the 5th January 2019.

Greg Almond
January 2019

CONTENTS

INTRODUCTION: AIMS OF THIS PRACTICAL GUIDE

This entry level, practical guide is addressed to the client/consumer. The style and format should help the practitioner to understand the key issues and *key practice points* that are included for the lawyers' benefit.

Case law is included to provide examples.

As this is an entry level guide, I suggest further detailed research is undertaken prior to accepting new instructions in this area.

Growing industry

Men, women and even children (unbelievably) are embracing the beauty treatment revolution, whether at home or in a local salon.

One in three (33% of) Britons have received a treatment in either a spa, salon or other treatment area in the past 12 months – an increase from 30% in 2015, according to *Mintel's Spa, Salon and In-Store Treatments UK 2017 Report*. UK consumers are estimated to spend £7.6 billion on treatments in spa, salons and in-store treatment areas in 2017, which is expected to rise to £8 billion by 2021.

In addition to this, the 'do it yourself' beauty treatment market is booming! Home hair dye kits, waxing products and permanent make up are to name just a few rising trends. As such, claims arising from negligent beauty treatment or products are becoming more commonplace as the industry grows.

Injuries

When beauty treatments do go wrong, they can cause severe injuries both physically and mentally. The injuries caused can last many years in certain cases and sometimes can be extremely personal.

It is essential for the practitioner to build and maintain a close working relationship with your client; empathy is essential. A greater understanding of the treatments and process will help put your client at ease.

Aim of this book

The primary aim of this book is to assist the personal injury practitioner when considering new enquiries and dealing with beauty claims – it is an entry level guide.

It will be especially useful for practitioners who have not undertaken this work before and are looking to expand their service offering.

As such, in Part One of the book, I will describe common beauty treatments with a brief explanation as to how they should be performed by a competent practitioner. Key practice notes will be provided.

This section will also address the common problems and how to help your client pursue a claim for compensation avoiding the pitfalls.

Part Two is intended to be a practical guide for practitioners and will include a sample client questionnaire and risk assessment checklist. I will also consider patch testing, claims involving children, disclosure and public liability insurance issues. There is also a chapter discussing cosmetic surgery claims.

I hope this guide will assist as a useful resource to personal injury practitioners when dealing with beauty negligence claims.

PART ONE

COMMON BEAUTY TREATMENTS AND PROBLEMS

CHAPTER ONE
TYPES OF BEAUTY TREATMENTS AND RISKS

The most common beauty treatments are as follows:

HAIR REMOVAL

WAXING

Bikini waxing, including Brazilian wax is the removal of hair growth in sensitive parts of the lower body.

Risks: The areas of skin that are treated are highly sensitive on the body and susceptible to damage. Hot wax used during these treatments can cause injuries such as burns, cuts or infections if poorly applied, or handled incorrectly.

LASER HAIR REMOVAL

Uses a powerful laser or 'intense pulsed light' (IPL) to remove unwanted hair. This light source heats and destroys hair follicles in the skin, which disrupts hair growth. Common areas to treat are the face, legs, arms, underarms and bikini line.

Risks: Crusting or blistering of the skin, scarring, excessive swelling, bruising, burns, or a rare condition called 'livedo reticularis', where skin becomes mottled.

SKIN

SUNBEDS

Sunbed tanning and the application of fake tan provides a healthy glow and sunbeds offer an excellent source of vitamin D.

Risks: Some people suffer an allergic reaction to fake tan. Over-exposure to UV rays can cause burns, or damage to the eyes such as conjunctivitis and cataracts. The overuse of sunbeds can also cause skin cancer.

CHEMICAL PEELS

A procedure that involves liquid being brushed onto the face to remove dead skin cells and stimulate the growth of new cells.

Risks: Potentially permanent darkening or lightening of the skin, infection or cold sores.

DERMA ROLLER

The skin is penetrated by microneedles attached to a roller to try and improve complexion.

Risks: Derma rollers that are not properly sterilised may transmit bacteria and diseases between clients, causing infections. Allergic reactions to either the anaesthetic used on the skin, or the roller's microneedles are another possibility and a patch test should be carried out. Poor technique may cause skin damage or permanent scarring.

MICRODERMABRASION

Using a vacuum, fine crystals are blasted to remove dead skin cells from the face, eradicating minor blemishes or lines.

Risks: If the application device is not handled by a qualified technician the microcrystals may penetrate the skin and break capillaries. Hyperpigmentation, where the skin has patches of lighter or dark might also occur. It is also possible for the crystals to enter the eyes, or if inhaled can have an impact on breathing.

DERMAL FILLERS

Dermal fillers are injections to get rid of wrinkles or creases in the skin.

Risks: Infection, swelling, itching, the filler can move, the formation of lumps (requiring surgery or medication), and in the worst cases a blood vessel can get blocked, leading to tissue death, blindness, or a pulmonary embolism.

BOTOX

Botulinum toxin injections are treatments that can also be used to help relax facial muscles, reducing the appearance of lines and wrinkles.

Risks: Flu-like symptoms, bruising, temporary droopiness of the face, breathing problems or blurred vision.

TATTOOS

A tattoo is a permanent inking of the skin using needles.

Risks: Allergic reaction or infection. Hepatitis B, Hepatitis C, or HIV if the equipment is not properly sterilised. Future MRI exams may also be affected, due to the pigments altering the quality of the image.

CHAPTER TWO
HAIRDRESSER
NEGLIGENCE

This chapter covers:

- Hygiene procedures

- Injuries

- Case Law

- The safety of stylists

- Patch testing

- Registration

Hygiene procedures

A spotless, safe salon gives a positive impression to customers. Salons should be kept impeccably clean, with floors and surfaces immaculate. Salon staff should wear clean clothing or overalls, they should ensure they always have washed their hands and any cuts should be properly covered with plasters.

Strict hygiene regulations should be in place and all equipment used needs to be thoroughly sterilised, such as combs, brushes, scissors and razors. Infections and viruses can easily spread between clients such as flu, dermatitis and scalp ringworm (causing scaly and bald patches to form on the scalp). Another major concern is impetigo, a bacterial skin infection causing painful blisters on the skin, face and hands. More seriously, hepatitis B, hepatitis C and HIV could be transmitted due to poor hygiene.

All implements should be clean and sanitised, especially due to the fact that if a stylist has an accident and cuts a client with scissors, then bodily fluids that transmit infections could be exposed. It is the duty of the salon owner to ensure all staff adhere to health and safety Regulations.

Relevant health and safety warnings, posters, guidance should be displayed in staff areas and in the staff handbook or employee contract. Health and safety should form part of inductions for new staff and be assessed on a regular basis.

Irrespective of the volume of clients they may tend to on a daily basis, clients expect their safety to be paramount even if they haven't considered the risks associated with attending the salon.

Injuries

The most common injuries that usually occur in hair salons are accidental cuts from scissors or razors, allergic reactions to the chemicals used and burns from electrical appliances. Cases of 'beauty parlour syndrome' have also been recorded, where the neck is put into an awkward position while in the sink, which can be fatal.

A traumatic salon experience does not only cause physical damage, but there is also emotional trauma involved. You may suffer from low self-esteem or embarrassment if you are unhappy with your transformation – meaning your work, or social life may be significantly affected.

CASE LAW

Smith v Hair Associates

General damages

£7250.00

PSLA

Value Today

General Damages £9748.37

Injuries sustained: chemical burns to scalp, permanent patches of baldness, psychological damage, mild adjustment disorder (CBT recommended)

Case Summary

The Claimant (aged 17 at the time of incident) attended the hair salon in July 2007 receiving a treatment which resulted in chemical burns to her scalp.

Following this, she had a skin graft on her scalp and was diagnosed with a mild adjustment disorder. Cognitive behavioural therapy has also been recommended to aid with this disorder.

She has been left with areas on her scalp where hair will never grow.

Details of Events

On 17th August 2007 the Claimant attended a hair salon owned by the named Defendant. The treatment intended was a half head of highlights, a treatment previously experienced by the Claimant. However, this was the Claimant's first time attending the Defendant's salon.

A patch test was not carried out on the Claimant prior to treatment.

As the highlight solutions and foils were applied to the hair, the Claimant immediately felt a burning sensation at the rear of her head. Concerned, the Claimant reached back to touch the area, finding the foils to be extremely hot.

At this point, the Claimant requested that the foils already placed be removed. The hairdresser refused, assuring the Claimant that everything was fine.

A further couple of minutes passed and the burning feeling became stronger, the Claimant again requested that the foils be removed. This time, the hair dresser complied. As she began to remove the initial foils from the Claimant's hair the stylist appeared to burn her hands, donning gloves to remove the remaining foils.

Once the solutions have been washed from the hair, the Claimant noticed that clumps of hair were missing from her scalp. The salon manager came to inspect the hair, suggesting that it was fine. At the managers instruction, the Claimant's hair was dried and styled.

No aftercare or advice was provided.

After leaving the salon, the Claimant returned to her home and asked her mother to look at the back of her head. Her mother noticed blisters on the scalp. They returned to the salon later in the day, however it was closed.

The Claimant faced discomfort over the following few days, noting the patch of skin was painful.

In August 2007 she visited her GP who prescribed antibiotics. It was found she had suffered burns to her head and hair loss.

In September 2017, the Claimant was referred to a specialist burns unit for treatment. The area affected had expanded to approximately 5x8cm. Further hair loss was also discovered in the surrounding areas.

The Claimant underwent a skin graft procedure.

The Claimant pursued a claim for damages for the injuries and suffering caused by the alleged negligence by the Defendant. It is unknown whether it was a product or lack of care in handling of products that caused the burn.

Liability was admitted by the Defendant

The Claimant was left with a significant bald patch (5x8cm) at the back of her head that required further treatment.

It was recommended that she undergo a serial excision procedure, this would help to treat the hair loss and scarring. The procedure involved numerous operations to obtain a skin graft, ultimately leaving her with a horizontal scar at the back of her head.

A Psychiatric report confirmed psychological damage relating to confidence. She was also diagnosed with a mild adjustment disorder. Cognitive behavioural therapy was recommended to help with her confidence and self-image.

KEY PRACTICE NOTE

The Defendant didn't carry out a patch test, or ask the client to complete a questionnaire.

It is always worth asking your client if they were required to complete a 'health/new client' questionnaire – sometimes this is simply a box ticking exercise and the questionnaire isn't even reviewed. Was your client emailed a copy?

No aftercare was provided by the salon.

Would appropriate aftercare have reduced swelling, redness etc…? If it had been advised, did your client follow the advice?

Liability was obviously admitted in this case.

Good quality photographs are essential, remind clients to preserve evidence.

Collect hair that has fallen out and take regular, high quality photographs.

Always consider the psychological effects.

The safety of stylists

Although the salon and stylist may have followed every procedure correctly to ensure the customer is safe, it is important to remember that the stylists are putting themselves at risk on a daily basis. Simple activities such as cutting and washing hair and using hairspray can all cause serious health implications. Stylists should always wear gloves and ensure they have taken regular breaks.

There is also the possibility that breathing in dangerous chemicals could be linked to asthma, in 2003 research proved that in France 20% of female asthma sufferers worked in the hairdressing industry. Dermatitis, a condition which can be caused by having hands in water regularly is also another major concern, research again proving that a staggering almost three quarters of hair stylists have reported suffering from a skin condition during their career.

More seriously, tendonitis and arthritis are also possibilities. Some parallels have been drawn between hair dye and bladder cancer and research carried out in 2010 suggested that hairdressers are more at risk than other people. However, Cancer Research UK suggested this was perhaps more applicable to stylists who worked with hair dye chemicals that have now been discontinued.

KEY PRACTICE NOTE

Remember such claims are likely to be employers' liability claims, starting in the portal.

If self employed by the salon, check the client's agreement or contract. If your client works in other salons causation can be an issue.

Ask lifestyle questions; potential other causes of the dermatitis?

Patch Testing

It is imperative that a skin patch test is always carried out to identify if the customer has an allergy to any of the chemicals used. Under 'Section 3 of the Health & Safety at Work Act' a patch test is legally required, failure to do so can result in prosecution. 24 hours prior to receiving a colouring treatment in the salon a patch test needs to be done, even if an 'organic' colour has been selected, although there is no ammonia in the product there may be something else that could cause an allergic reaction. *Did the salon discuss a patch test when you booked the appointment?*

The offer of a hair strand test should also be made available, particularly if you have previously bleached your hair to ensure the product will not cause future breakage. It is important to remember that even if you have had the same treatment in the past, chemicals in the product could have been changed by the manufacturer, or you may have developed an allergy to something new, so a patch test should be carried out every single time to be safe.

Some hair straightening procedures also require a strand test to be completed 48 hours before to check the strength of hair and to ensure that it will be able to cope with the level of chemical treatment that is going to be used. Formaldehyde is usually used in straightening procedures and this chemical could trigger a reaction, so it is imperative to always check beforehand.

When visiting a hair salon clients trust that their stylist is an experienced professional who has carried out similar treatments before. Often the worst injuries occur as a result of inexperienced or junior stylists who are incompetent at mixing hair colour to the desired strength, often because they do not have the qualifications or training required to do this. Serious damage can also occur if the chemical has not been taken off the hair at the optimum time, this can cause thinning of the hair and future hair loss.

The hairdressing industry is the second most at risk occupation for working with hazardous chemicals. The 'Control of Substances Hazardous to Health Regulations 2002' (COSHH) requires that salons store and dispose of chemicals properly, for example perming lotion. Inhaling dangerous fumes from the products, or if a chemical comes into contact with the eyes or skin are the most common problems, so it is important that stylists are vigilant and follow all of the correct procedures. Chemicals should have correct ventilation and an organised system should be in place in case a spillage was to occur. *Are the products labelled clearly and does the salon look organised and well maintained?*

Hair salons also use a lot of electrical equipment such as hair dryers, straightening irons and curling wands, 'The Provision and Use of Work Equipment Regulations 1998' requests that these are also tested to ensure the safety of both the client and the stylist.

Registration

The hair and beauty industry employ around a quarter of a million people in the UK. There are around 36,000 hair salons and the industry is thriving. Although a monumental industry, it is not regulated and this unfortunately allows stylists to work who do not have the correct experience or qualifications. The number of mobile hair and beauty stylists are also increasing. For some reason the UK does not have a system of compulsory registration. This is appalling given the size of the industry and the potential danger to employees and customers.

The Hairdressers (Registration) Act 1964 allows hairdressers to register with the Hairdressing Council (https://www.haircouncil.org.uk/) voluntarily, but shockingly only 5% actually do this. Before visiting a salon carry out research and check they have a certificate displayed to prove they are a registered establishment.

Over the years chemicals in the products used in hair salons have changed, this combined with intense heat means that hair salon customers are vulnerable to injury, especially if the stylist has not received the correct level of training. Salons and stylists are aware they are dealing with dangerous products and due to this it is imperative they have taken out adequate insurance cover, to protect both them, the business and their customers.

KEY PRACTICE NOTE

Insurance

Does the salon have adequate insurance?

Did your client receive any paperwork from the salon? Did they notice a certificate of insurance in the reception?

I have found the lack of insurance to be a major issue when pursuing claims. It is vital for your ongoing risk assessment that the Defendant is adequately insured and able to satisfy the claim.

Training

Do you know the training credentials of the stylist?

I have seen many different certificates from an array of so-called 'professional bodies'. Investigate if this is a legitimate provider.

When did the stylist last attend a training session?

Does the salon offer in-house training sessions?

Consider the above questions prior to requesting pre-action disclosure.

Each case is different and needs to be thoroughly researched. Although there is no guarantee when visiting a hair salon that everything will go smoothly, customers still demand an excellent duty of care and should feel they are in safe hands. Clients trust that all of the required health and safety procedures have been adhered to and put themselves in a vulnerable position. Clients can often be rushing under time restraints.

Sometimes clients will be under the impression they have grounds for a case if they are dissatisfied with the 'transformation' they have received, but obviously a hair salon is not required to pay compensation in this instance.

Most salons will attempt to rectify the problem. However, has the trust and confidence gone?

It is the duty of the salon owner to ensure all staff adhere to health and safety Regulations.

Relevant health and safety warnings, posters, guidance should be displayed in staff areas and in the staff handbook or employee contract. Health and safety should form part of inductions for new staff and be assessed on a regular basis.

Irrespective of the volume of clients they may tend to on a daily basis; clients expect their safety to be paramount even if they haven't considered the risks associated with attending the salon.

KEY PRACTICE NOTE

Below is relevant legislation to consider.

This is in summary form and should be considered prior to undertaking this work.

Did the service fall below the standard expected?

Know your client – is this is a genuine personal injury claim, or a disgruntled client?

Will the injury be cost bearing? Civil Liberties Bill, small claims increase to 2k?

If an injury does occur, the employment status of the stylist will be investigated because they might be liable. Some salons employ self-employed stylists, so both the individual stylist and the salon could have separate insurance. Early disclosure is key, ensure your CNF has a complete disclosure list of relevant documents.

As in all cases, expert evidence is vital to ensure your client's claim is successful. The input of a trichologist (a hair and scalp specialist) may be necessary. Please see Part Two of this guide for recommended experts. Building relationships with an expert can be very useful, so identify the appropriate expert. Reviewing GP records is essential. Prepare a summary and chronology. Has the client suffered with a reaction before? Is this documented? Obtain the client's comments.

We will discuss expert evidence in Part Two.

CHAPTER THREE
HAIR DYE AT HOME AND
IN THE SALON – CAMPAIGN
AGAINST PPD

This chapter covers:

- Why do some people have a reaction?

- Avoiding a reaction

- Signs of a reaction

- What to do if you have a reaction

- PPD

- Campaign against PPD

- Consumer Protection Act 1987

- Case law

Why do some people have a reaction?

Some people have sensitive skin and therefore are susceptible to contact dermatitis, meaning their skin can get inflamed when they make contact with a substance that causes irritation. The substance may cause a physical reaction on the skin, or it may act as an allergen, which could lead to a much more serious and sometimes even fatal reaction.

Due to the ingredients that hair dyes consist of, many can irritate your skin or cause a severe allergic reaction. Education on the risks of hair dye and knowing what to do in case of an emergency is important and if the correct safety advice is followed, in most cases they are completely avoidable.

The main culprit for triggering allergic reactions through the use of hair dye is the chemical paraphenylenediamine, often referred to as 'PPD'.

Avoiding a reaction

The most efficient way of avoiding having an allergic reaction is by carrying out a patch test. If you are using a salon then they should do this for you, but if you are carrying out the procedure at home then you need to do your own. A patch test should be carried out every single time, even if it is the same dye you always use because an ingredient might have changed, or you could have developed an allergy to something new. Dab a tiny bit of the dye either behind your ear or on your inner elbow and wait for it to dry. Monitor your skin and check if there is any reaction – if you notice there is, or you feel unwell then do not use the product. If you want to be extra vigilant you can visit an allergy clinic and request a test to find out if you are allergic to any chemicals and will then know to avoid these in the future.

If the patch test is successful and you do not have any irritation then you can proceed to use the product. However, always read the instructions thoroughly and wear gloves to protect your skin.

Do not leave the dye on for longer than the recommended time and always remember to rinse your hair.

KEY PRACTICE NOTE

Patch test every time!

Did your client carry out the patch test on this occasion? Make sure you have clear instructions.

Clients often will rely on a patch test carried out on a previous occasion whether at home or at the salon. (Sometimes not always at the same salon.)

Evidence is vital – witnesses – did a partner, friend or family member witness your client carrying out the patch test, or remember you referring to the patch test? A statement early in the case can pay dividends.

Signs of a reaction

Depending on the individual, the reaction to PPD can either be mild, such as irritation in the scalp, or it could cause a life-threatening allergic reaction. A mild irritation to PPD might feel like your skin is burning and the scalp, neck, forehead, ears or eyelids might become inflamed, sometimes it can take up to 2 days for visible mild side effects to occur.

However, if you have a severe reaction to PPD you may notice straight away and your scalp might itch and your face could even start to swell. In the very worst cases the body can start to go into 'anaphylactic shock', a frightening and potentially fatal reaction. Signs of anaphylactic shock are if the mouth starts to swell and breathing becomes obstructed. The eyes may become heavily swollen, as well as the lips, hands and feet. Anaphylaxis will make you feel very unwell, you may be lightheaded or nauseous and in the worst cases you could collapse and fall unconscious.

What to do if you have a reaction

Without hesitation you must call for an ambulance if you are worried that you have the symptoms of anaphylactic shock. For mild reactions, rinse your hair and wash it with a gentle shampoo and then carefully massage a moisturising cream into the skin to ease irritation. You may require a steroid cream, which you will be able to get from either a pharmacist or GP.

PPD

'PPD' is a chemical called paraphenylenediamine and is the main cause of reactions to hair dye. Severe reactions are rare and as long as the instructions have been read carefully and an adequate patch test has been completed, then PPD is otherwise perfectly safe, as the level of chemical in the product is limited. It is important to note that black henna tattoos also contain PPD, so if you have had one in the past or have one at the time of using the hair dye then you are making yourself even more vulnerable to having a reaction.

Any type of reaction should be taken seriously and you should refrain from using anything that contains PPD. There are other hair colouring products that are PPD free, so these are a sensible option. However, it's important to read the instructions as irritation could still be possible.

Campaign against PPD

Under European law the use of PPD is allowed in the UK, however its use has previously been restricted in other European countries, such as Germany, France and Sweden.

There is a strong campaign against the use of PPD and a call for it to be banned over fear of severe allergic reactions. I have urged the government for many years to re-consider the use of PPD after representing several clients who believe that hair dyes have caused them to suffer extreme allergic reactions.

The tragic death of Tabatha McCourt, a 17-year-old teenager who died after suffering a seizure 20 minutes after using a hair dye kit at home intensified this campaign.

The Cosmetic Toiletry and Perfumery Association (CTPA) stated that an allergic reaction to PPD can "develop over time, which is why a skin allergy test must be carried out each time the hair is to be coloured". However, they also added "European commission scientists' opinion is that PPD is safe for use as a hair dye, and its use is strictly regulated. At this time, PPD cannot be replaced in hair colourants: nothing else is as effective and it is safe when used as directed."

Following Tabatha's death, I directly appealed to the business minister at the time, Edward Davey, and suggested introducing a ban on the use of PPD in the UK. A Department of Business, Innovation and Skills spokesperson stated: "This is obviously a terrible tragedy, but we need to know for certain what caused Tabatha's death. Such severe reactions are extremely rare. However, it's important that hair dye users read and follow the safety instructions accompanying a product before use."

Another of my clients received a pre-issue settlement from a reputable large cosmetics firm after informing them she had suffered a severe reaction. Despite thoroughly reading the instructions and carrying out the required patch test, her scalp began itching and she went into anaphylactic shock.

The campaign against the use of PPD is gaining momentum. Other cases include Marina Williamson, a London based lawyer who carried out a successful patch test and proceeded to use a home hair dye. A couple of days later she encountered a severe skin reaction, terrifying breathing problems and her heart rate was severely raised.

I believe despite the CTPA's position the manufacturers of hair dye products are aware of the potential issues. I don't believe the reactions are as rare as they 'the manufacturers' state/ argue but there currently isn't sufficient data. One of my clients received a pre-issue settlement from a reputable large cosmetics from after informing them she had suffered a severe reaction. Despite thoroughly reading the instructions and carrying out the required patch test, her scalp began itching and she went into anaphylactic shock.

Consumer Protection Act 1987

Legislation to consider, Consumer Protection Act 1987 Section 3. If the court is satisfied that the safety of the product was "not such as persons generally were entitled to expect" you are likely to succeed with your claim. You would need to prove that it was the product that caused injury or loss and that you followed all of the required guidelines, as the manufacturer will be successful if they can prove there was no known defect at the time the product was supplied.

KEY PRACTICE NOTE

The Defendant is likely to request the box which contained the product, so that the batch number can be tested.

Does your client have the box or even better the product itself?

Ask them to retain all evidence and it might be worth undertaking your own expert testing of the product. However, this can be expensive and will be depend on the nature of the case.

The Defendant will run a test against the sample from the batch number you provide.

It is also worth checking if the product in question has been recalled.

https://www.tradingstandards.uk/consumers/product-recalls

CONSUMER PROTECTION ACT 1987

https://www.legislation.gov.uk/ukpga/1987/43

Meaning of "defect"

(1) Subject to the following provisions of this section, there is a defect in a product for the purposes of this part if the safety of the product is not such as persons generally are entitled to expect; and for those purposes "safety", in relation to a product, shall include safety with respect to products comprised in that product and safety in the context of risks of damage to property, as well as in the context of risks of death or personal injury.

(2) In determining for the purposes of subsection (1) above what persons generally are entitled to expect in relation to a product all the circumstances shall be taken into account, including—

(a) The manner in which, and purposes for which, the product has been marketed, its get-up, the use of any mark in relation to the product and any instructions for, or warnings with respect to, doing or refraining from doing anything with or in relation to the product;

(b) What might reasonably be expected to be done with or in relation to the product; and

(c) The time when the product was supplied by its producer to another; and nothing in this section shall require a defect to be inferred from the fact alone that the safety of a product which is supplied after that time is greater than the safety of the product in question.

CASE LAW

AB v TREVOR SORBIE INTERNATIONAL PLC (2016)

Total Damages: £9,500 (£10,380.58 RPI)

PSLA: £7,500 (£8,195.19 RPI)

Trial/settlement date: 21/2/2016

Type of Award: Out of Court Settlement

Age at trial: 45

Court: Out of Court Settlement

Age at injury: 42

Sex: Female

The Claimant secured £9,500.00 for injuries sustained at a hairdressing salon.

A hair dye solution was left on the Claimant's scalp for an excessive amount of time, causing a reaction which developed into irritant dermatitis. This then caused widespread dermatitis, beyond just the scalp, due to an underlying form of eczema.

On 27 October 2012, the Claimant attended the Defendant's hairdressing salon to receive a hair dying treatment. The dye applied to the hair was left on for an extended amount of time, causing her scalp to react and become dry and itchy shortly after.

This reaction soon developed into irritant dermatitis and later caused dermatitis to spread across her entire body. An underlying endogenous eczema brought on this spread of dermatitis when triggered by the irritant dermatitis.

The Claimant claimed damages against the Defendant for the injuries suffered, alleging they were negligent in failing to manage the treatment timing correctly.

Liability was admitted by the Defendant.

Injuries: The Claimant suffered an initial reaction on her scalp which ultimately developed into dermatitis across her entire body.

Total injury duration: 3 years

Effects:

The widespread dermatitis would settle after 3 years with the use of a steroid cream.

Out of Court Settlement: £9,500, total damages

Breakdown of General Damages: Pain, suffering and loss of amenity: £7,500.

Simmons v Castle [2012] EWCA Civ 1288 10 per cent uplift: applied.

Special Damages: £2,000.

KEY PRACTICE NOTE

The Defendant didn't carry out a patch test. It is vital to establish a clear version and chronology of events from your client to establish liability.

The application of hair dye must be in accordance with the manufacturer's instructions. Carefully reviewing the hair dye instructions provided by the manufacturer is very important. Do you have a copy?

If not, include in your pre-action disclosure request to the defendant. Check the packaging. Has the Defendant changed the instructions? If so why?

CHAPTER FOUR
WAXING, TINTING,
TATTOOS, PIERCING,
CHEMICAL PEELS
& SUNBEDS

<u>Waxing</u>

Bikini and Brazilian waxing are popular procedures that many women opt for to remove unwanted hair growth from intimate areas. It takes around half an hour and leaves clients with 8 weeks of no hair growth.

A typically common waxing injury occurs when the beautician removes the strips of wax too early or too quickly, which can cause the skin to tear and bleed. This can be painful, irritating and can cause in growing hairs – if the client has a holiday planned, then it would be entirely spoilt and loss of sexual desire would also be another important aspect to consider.

Another complication can be if the wax is not heated at the desired temperature, serious lasting damage such as burns may ensue. Failure to follow strict sanitisation guidelines can result in infection and a traumatic experience could cause significant emotional damage and embarrassment. Beauticians must be fully qualified to carry out waxing procedures and impeccable hygiene standards should be met to reduce the risk of infection.

Tinting

Eyebrow and eyelash tinting are growing trends that simple involve a beautician carefully applying a semi-permanent dye to the area. It is a popular treatment for people who have dyed their hair and want their eyebrow colour to match, or if they want to create definition. An eyebrow tint takes around 20-25 minutes and the beautician will apply a petroleum jelly on the surrounding skin to avoid it staining, before carefully applying the dye.

Eyelash tinting is a similar procedure and gives the appearance of thicker lashes without the need to wear mascara. The beautician will protect your eyes before applying the dye, it will then be left to set into the eyelashes for between 5-10 minutes and will last between 4-6 weeks.

Due to the close proximity of the eyes, it is vital that only a fully qualified technician administers the treatment and a patch test should be carried out 24 hours before. Common problems can be skin irritation, swelling and in rare cases, blindness.

Tattoos

A tattoo is a permanent inking on your skin with pigments that are inserted into the top layer through a tattoo gun, which pierces the skin. Every time a puncture is made tiny droplets of ink are absorbed into the skin.

Rigorous hygiene and sanitisation procedures are required when tattooing a client. Failure to correctly sterilise equipment can result in contracting hepatitis B, hepatitis C or HIV. It is important that an autoclave is used to clean equipment, as well as the tattooist wearing gloves. Common side effects can be allergic reactions and sometimes a granulomatous reaction can occur due to the pigments in the ink. The establishment should also be fully registered and licensed.

Piercings

Body and facial piercings are punctures made in the skin by a needle, jewellery can then be worn in places such as the ears, nose, lips or, bellybutton and many other locations.

Strict hygiene procedures should be adhered to, including the correct sanitisation of the equipment used to prevent the spreading of hepatitis B, hepatitis C and HIV.

Some people do encounter problems after getting a piercing such as an infection, the skin may tear or scar and an allergic reaction to the metal jewellery used is another possibility. The person carrying out the piercing should be fully qualified.

Chemical Peels

Chemical peeling involves the application of a liquid to the skin, which is then peeled off to expose a fresh new layer of skin underneath and to build collagen. There are 3 levels and the deep chemical peel carries the most risk. Skin can become swollen or red and a local anaesthetic may be required and due to the chemical used. It is important that the heart and blood pressure are checked, as these can be affected during a treatment.

Sunbeds

Sunbeds enable users to maintain a healthy all year-round tan and roughly 3 million people in the UK use them. It is a straight forward procedure and involves standing or lying down and exposing your skin to UV rays, similar to those from the sun.

There are risks with using sunbeds and common injuries can include burns to the skin, or the irritation of eye conditions such as conjunctivitis or cataracts. Skin cancer is also a huge risk as it has been proven to be a contributing factor. It is important tanning salons provide accurate advice to clients, such as advising them how long they should spend on the sunbed.

CHAPTER FIVE
BOTOX AND DERMAL FILLERS

Botox

Botox injections are a popular procedure used to enhance the skin and to get rid of unwanted lines and wrinkles. Botulinum toxin has to be prescribed and should only be administered by a fully qualified professional. Sessions last around 10 minutes and can be done without the use of anaesthetic. It can take a few days before you see the results and it will last between 4 and 6 months, top up treatments will be required after this.

Side effects can be pain, bruising, swelling, fever, certain parts of the face may droop, vision can be affected and occasionally, breathing difficulties can occur. Pregnant or breast-feeding women should not undergo the treatment.

Dermal Fillers

Similar to Botox, Dermal fillers are also injections given to smooth the skin and to help get rid of unwanted lines and wrinkles on the face, they can also be injected into the lips and cheeks to enhance them. The injections contain either collagen, hyaluronic acid, calcium hydroxylapatite, poly-L-lactic acid, or polymethylmethacrylate beads and can last between 3 months and 2 years, depending on which filler you have opted for. Although it is a relatively painless procedure, you might be offered a local anaesthetic cream or injection.

Common side effects can be swelling, bruising, infection, the filler can move from where it was originally injected into and lumps may form. Although rare, there is also the risk that a filler can obstruct a blood vessel.

It is important that you thoroughly research the clinic and practitioner before undergoing either of these treatments.

Check the establishment has been legally registered, read reviews from past clients and make sure you are confident that it is safe and hygienic and all of the correct procedures to keep you safe have been put into action.

Ensure that a consultation is held prior to your appointment to discuss the procedure in detail, the practitioner should want to know your full medical history and make sure you have educated yourself on what could go wrong, or the possible side effects.

It is important to note there are no guarantees with any treatment and it might not turn out exactly as you had envisaged. Claims are for negligence not for dissatisfaction with the service.

CHAPTER SIX
PRODUCT LIABILITY

Manufacturers of products have an obligation to ensure they are safe. Neglect on their part could result in a legal case against them being pursued and the company could be sued for injury or death, sometimes resulting in either a fine or imprisonment. Suppliers of products also have to take responsibility for what they are selling because they are the ones providing it to the general public.

Products should be safe before they are sold and need to have gone through the required testing procedures. Any potential risks or dangers should be clearly labelled on the product, if this is not done correctly then the manufacturer is liable.

Trading Standards monitor the safety of products and have the power to check and cease any items they deem unsafe. They are permitted to take action if they are not satisfied and can decide to either order you to stop selling the item immediately, request legally that the product is destroyed, recall the item in question, or they can decide to prosecute you in the most serious cases.

KEY PRACTICE NOTE

It is worth reviewing the following relevant legalisation:

Consumer protection act 1987

https://www.legislation.gov.uk/ukpga/1987/43

Consumer Rights Act 2015

http://www.legislation.gov.uk/ukpga/2015/15/contents/enacted

CHAPTER SEVEN
CONTACT DERMATITIS – HAIRDRESSER

This chapter covers:

- Who is at risk?

- What is dermatitis?

- Prevention

- Raising Awareness

- Treatment

- Emollients

- Side effects

- Topical Corticosteroids

- Steroids

- Referral

Who is at risk?

Hair stylists are highly likely to suffer from dermatitis throughout their career, with 7 out of 10 stylists reporting they are victims of this. Hair colourant, bleach, perm solutions, shampoos and cleaning products can have an adverse effect on skin, meaning that as a precaution most stylists now opt to wear gloves to protect themselves. Stylists who have an extreme reaction often have to sadly end their careers, as it is impossible to work on a daily basis with the condition. It is important to note that care must always be taken, as the majority of home beauty and household products often contain identical chemicals to those found in salons.

It is not just the chemicals that can cause dermatitis, another major contributor is working with the hands in water for long periods of time. 'Wet washers' do not just work in hair salons – cleaners, kitchen staff, caterers and those working as car washers often spend around two hours a day with their hands submersed in water and are putting themselves at risk of triggering contact dermatitis.

What is dermatitis?

It is a common skin disorder that occurs in two different types – irritant contact, or allergic contact dermatitis. The main symptoms of it are itchy, red, dry, flaking or cracked skin and in some cases painful blisters can appear.

Irritant contact dermatitis can be caused by certain chemicals, such as those found in soaps or detergent, but more commonly it develops over time by working frequently with the hands in water. People who suffer from eczema are also more likely to be susceptible to this.

Allergic contact dermatitis commonly usually occurs when you have spent long periods of time with the skin exposed to certain chemicals. However, those with sensitive skin may find they have a reaction immediately. Suffering from allergic contact dermatitis means you will always suffer from the same allergy in the future.

Prevention

Wear disposable, non-latex gloves when using bleach, colourant, shampoo or water. The majority of salons have established that long length non-latex gloves are the best, but should be changed for each customer. Latex gloves are not recommended due to the fact clients could be allergic to latex, a condition that can prove fatal.

Monitor your skin and regularly check for any symptoms such as dryness, redness or itchiness. Remember to always dry your hands well and moisturise at the start of each day and after you have washed your hands. Moisturise thoroughly, remembering to rub it into the fingertips and wrists. Fragrance free moisturisers are usually recommended for sensitive skin. Aqueous or paraffin-based creams are advisable for dermatitis and other skin conditions because they help to prevent dryness and cracking.

KEY PRACTICE NOTE

Your client is likely to be a hairdresser or employee at the salon; remember to ask key questions regarding:

Training – what training was provided? Was there regular updated training, especially in relation to products and equipment.

Contract – do you have a copy of your client's contract? Is there a salon manual outlining risk assessment?

Review GP records early - summary and chronology required such as, previous incidents and treatment. How long has your client been a hairdresser, or worked in salons?

Link to legalisation:

Personal Protective Equipment at Work Regulations 1992

http://www.legislation.gov.uk/uksi/1992/2966/contents/made

Disclosure

Personal Protective Equipment at Work Regulations 1992

    i.   *Documents relating to the assessment of the Personal Protective Equipment to comply with Regulation 6;*

    ii.   *Documents relating to the maintenance and replacement of Personal Protective Equipment to comply with Regulation 7;*

iii. *Record of maintenance procedures for Personal Protective Equipment to comply with Regulation 7;*

iv. *Records of tests and examinations of Personal Protective Equipment to comply with Regulation 7;*

v. *Documents providing information, instruction and training in relation to the Personal Protective Equipment to comply with Regulation 9;*

vi. *Instructions for use of Personal Protective Equipment to include the manufacturers' instructions to comply with Regulation 10;*

Raising Awareness

'Bad Hand Day', a campaign designed to raise awareness of dermatitis and why gloves should be used was initiated in 2006. The famous Mark Hill, celebrity hairdresser agreed "Buying and wearing non-latex gloves to protect your hands from skin damage makes good business sense."

Following the campaign, the majority of salons now carry out frequent 'hand checks' once a month to enable stylists to check for any symptoms of dermatitis. Stylists who were previously reluctant to use gloves also soon saw the benefits after they were educated. Contact dermatitis is a serious condition that can have a detrimental impact on your life.

Treatment

The first step is to attempt to identify the product triggering the dermatitis and to avoid it, you should find that symptoms drastically improve and may even disappear. It can be difficult identifying what it is triggering your reaction, but a pharmacist, GP or dermatologist may be able to advise you further if you speak to them. Always wear protective clothing or gloves if your job requires you to come into contact with a product that triggers a reaction to reduce the risk.

Emollients

Your GP or pharmacist should be able to recommend a treatment, such as an emollient (moisturiser) to ease the reaction and prevent dryness. An emollient is applied directly to the skin in an attempt to reduce water loss and provide protection, eczema sufferers regularly use them.

There is a wide selection of emollients available, so it may be a case of trial and error to find one that works for you. You might find that your regular emollient is not working as well as usual, or is starting to cause irritation – in this instance enquire about different products as there are many available.

Sometimes a range of different emollients are recommended such as ointments, lotions and creams and they all have different amounts of oil in them. Creams and lotions are for less dry skin, with lotions containing the smallest amount of oil, these are usually recommended for inflamed or irritated skin.

Ointments are recommended for dry skin that is not inflamed – they are greasy, but very effective at moisturising the skin. Creams are usually in between a lotion and an ointment. There are also emollient products that can be used as an alternative to soap, separate ones to use on the face, hands and body, or a special emollient to use in the shower or to add into the bath.

Never share emollients with anyone else and if you are likely to come into contact with a product that will trigger your dermatitis, apply it regularly during and after work. A useful tip is to keep a separate supply at home and work. Apply a generous amount, smoothing it into the skin (not rubbing) and re-apply every 2 – 3 hours. Remember to use after a bath or shower after gently drying the skin and applying while it is still moist.

Side effects

Some emollients can irritate the skin, especially if you have contact dermatitis because your skin will be sensitive and may react to certain ingredients in the product. If this occurs, stop using the emollient and speak to your pharmacist who should be able to suggest an alternative. Never use emollients near a naked flame, due to some of them containing paraffin. Emollients added to bath water can also make your bath slippery, so be careful when climbing in and out.

Topical Corticosteroids

A topical corticosteroid (cream or ointment) is recommended if the skin is extremely inflamed, they are usually a safe and effective treatment that relieve symptoms within a few days. There are different types of topical corticosteroids, depending on which part of the body the reaction is in and the level of its severity. Weaker solutions are prescribed if the reaction is mild, or if it is in a sensitive area where the skin is not as thick such as, the face, genitals or elbows. Strong creams are usually recommended if the dermatitis is severe, or the reaction is on your palms or soles of the feet.

Read the instructions thoroughly and establish how much you need to apply and how frequently throughout the day the product should be used, always apply a thin layer. A corticosteroid is usually only applied once during the day and it should not be used more than twice. It can be used alongside your emollient; but wait around half an hour for the emollient to work before adding the topical corticosteroid. Depending on the strength of the product you are using then you are more at risk of encountering side effects. Try and use a small amount and the weakest product you can to control your dermatitis. Some typical side effects may be a slight burning when you apply it, increased hair growth, skin thinning, slight change in skin colour, or acne. Any side effects usually subside when you stop using the product.

Steroids

Corticosteroid tablets might be prescribed if you are suffering from a severe episode, or if a substantial area of your skin is inflamed. Usually steroid tablets are prescribed for around 1 week, but your dose might then be increased to 2 to 3 weeks if you are suffering from a bad episode.

Side effects:

Diabetes, hypertension, osteoporosis and reduced growth rate in children. Due to the extreme nature of the side effects your GP will most likely recommend you visit a specialist.

Referral

Your GP may decide to refer you to a dermatologist if they feel you need more advanced treatment. They may suggest you take alitretinoin, for severe eczema in the hands. Other treatments could be 'phototherapy', using UV light on the skin, or 'immunosuppressant therapy', medicines that suppress the immune system.

Alternative treatments

Herbal remedies and diet are sometimes used to treat contact dermatitis, but the effectiveness of these are unproved. Always discuss this with your GP first.

PART TWO

PRACTICAL GUIDE
FOR
PRACTITIONERS

CHAPTER EIGHT
PRACTICAL GUIDE: RUNNING A SUCCESSFUL CLAIM (VETTING / QUESTIONNAIRES / TACTICS / PORTAL / EXPERTS)

VETTING

Vetting new claims is extremely important in the new post Jackson/civil post liberties era.

Cases need to be vetted carefully by a senior member of the team.

Consider the Defendants ability to pay and the likely value of the claim.

As a guide I have implemented the following vetting procedure for my team:

- Senior solicitors to vet all new claims

- All new clients must be interviewed by phone, or in person

- Check social media of the potential client – with consent

- Check the status of the Defendant

- Funding check. Are you going to offer a CFA?

- Have a minimum threshold re quantum?

Ensure your client has been provided with clear advice regarding success fee deductions.

Have you trained your team regarding success fee deductions and risk assessments? Update training regarding costs on a regular basis; especially in terms of risk assessments.

Is the claim worth your minimum threshold? (2k/5k/10k)

We have a minimum threshold of £2k, but this is reviewed regularly and I would expect this to increase to £5k when the small claim limit changes.

Remember ATE – check current insurance policies.

Is your claim public liability, employers' liability, or a clinical negligence matter?

QUESTIONNAIRE

Full name	
Address	
Telephone (Mobile/Landline)	
Email address & Social Media Do you use social media? If so, please advise which accounts you use:	

Have you posted or commented regarding the injury?	
Date of birth	
NI Number	
Job title	
Employee/payroll number	
Employer's name and address	
Employer's telephone number	

Have you been absent from work? If yes, please provide the dates you were absent.	From: To:
If you are still off work, when do you plan on returning?	
Usual weekly or monthly wage?	
Loss of earnings? Please state your approximate loss on a weekly, or monthly basis for the period you were absent.	

ACCIDENT INFORMATION

Please provide us with as much information as you can about the accident.

Date and time of accident	
Location of accident	

Please describe in depth how the accident occurred and any relevant circumstances leading up to it. It is helpful if you can provide as much detail as possible – you can continue on additional sheets of paper, if necessary.

Was a patch/strand test offered or undertaken?

Did you complete any pre-treatment questionnaires (do you have a copy?)

Who do you think was responsible for the accident? Why?	

Do you have a copy of their insurance certificate? Can you obtain this?	
Do you think that you were in any way partly responsible for the accident?	
Is there any other inform-ation you think would be useful to us in estab-lishing who was responsible for your accident?	

Do you have the contact details of any other witnesses? Please provide contact details.	Name: Address: Telephone Number: What did they see?
	Name: Address: Telephone Number: What did they see?
Was the accident reported to anyone? For example, if it was at work was the employer made aware?	

DETAILS OF THE INJURIES YOU RECEIVED

What injuries did you sustain?

We require colour photographs of the injuries sustained and the products used, if possible.

If you are unable to take colour photographs, please advise us immediately and we will arrange for professional photographs to be taken.

When did you first realise you were injured?

Did you attend seek medical attention?

If so, please provide the name and address of the hospital, medical centre or doctor who examined you <u>AND</u> the appointment dates.

What treatment have you received?

Were you an inpatient? Is the treatment ongoing? If so, how many medical appointments have you had to attend as an out-patient?

Are you still suffering from your injuries?

If you have fully recovered from your injury please confirm how long the symptoms of the injury lasted.

Have the effects of the accident affected your ability to undertake everyday tasks? If so, please provide details.

If you participated in any sports or hobbies prior to the accident, has your ability to continue been affected by the accident?

If you are employed please provide details of any time you have had to take from work as a result of the accident. Have you incurred any expenses as a result of the accident?

Please complete the table below and add in any additional items that have caused you a loss.

Item of loss	Cost in £	Evidence in support (receipts etc...)	Evidence attached
Travel expenses			
Medication			
Initial treatment cost			

Aftercare or rectification treatment cost			
Property damage (include invoices)			
Other (give details)			

EXPERTS

As in any personal injury claim, selecting the right expert is crucial for the overall success of your client's claim – below are a selection of well-respected experts. I have included contact details which are accurate as at the date of writing.

The following experts are recommendations only. There are many suitable and very competent experts. The following are a selection.

(Please note the writer has no commercial arrangements with any of the listed experts)

TRICHOLOGIST

(Clinical *trichology* is the diagnosis and treatment of diseases and disorders of the human hair and scalp.)

Firm: HAIR SCIENTISTS UK

Job title: Consultant Trichologist
             (Hair & Scalp Expert 50 years)

Address: 19 Balgores Square
             Gidea Park
             Near Romford
             Essex
             England
             RM2 6AU

Email: admin@hairscientists.co.uk

Website: www.hairscientists.co.uk

For further information

https://www.trichologists.org.uk

Ensure experts are suitably accredited to undertake new instructions and have a good, working knowledge of the CPR and their responsibilities to the Court.

DERMATOLOGIST

Dermatology is the diagnosis and treatment of skin diseases, including acne, psoriasis, warts, skin infections and skin cancers.

Professor Andrew L Wright

Firm:	THE YORKSHIRE CLINIC
Job title:	Dermatologist
Telephone no:	01274 550600
Fax no:	01274 565349
Address:	Bradford Road Bingley West Yorkshire England BD16 1TW
Email address:	docwright1@hotmail.com

Dr Paul August, DERMATOLOGIST

SECRETARY: DEE SWINDLEHURST

01606 892522

PAUL.AUGUST@SKINDOC.CO.UK

Miss Sharon Stower

Firm:	SHARON STOWER CONSULTANCY LTD
Job title:	Nurse Expert and Independent Nursing and Healthcare Consultant
Telephone no:	01476 552125
Fax no:	01476 552125
Address:	39 High Street Swayfield Grantham Lincolnshire England NG33 4LL
Email:	sharon@sharonstower.com
Website:	www.sharonstower.com/consultancy.html

SKIN CAMOUFLAGE SERVICES

Mrs Vanessa Jane Davies MEWI, LCGI

Firm:	SKIN CAMOUFLAGE SERVICES LTD
Job title:	Skin Camouflage Consultant
Telephone no:	020 7467 8466
Address:	10 Harley Street London Greater London England W1G 9PF
Email:	vanessa@skincamouflageservices.co.uk
Website:	www.skincamouflageservices.co.uk
Qualifications:	University of Hertfordshire: Development of Skin Camouflage Practice. Huddersfield University: Certificate in Education. Licentiateship of The City & Guilds Institute.
Area of expertise:	Established in 2007, Skin Camouflage Services Ltd provide independent quantum expert reports based on past, current and future care. Clinical assessment for men women and children who are left with scars, burns and pigmentation resulting from trauma injuries. Competent in multiple injuries. Bond Solon Excellence in Report Writing and Courtroom Skills. CPD up to date.

TACTICS

Questionnaire

Ensure your client completes a very detailed questionnaire and sends you high quality photographs. Photographs need to be provided throughout the lifespan of the claim. Consider instructing a professional photographer.

I always ask my client to check and sign the initial questionnaire.

Records

Ask your client to obtain medical records from their GP at the outset. No cost in most circumstances.

Review, summarise and prepare a chronology.

Work with a quality medical agency. Please do not hesitate to contact me via my LinkedIn page for recommendations.

Funding

If you are offering your client a CFA, ensure you are content damages will be over £2000. If not, is it worth acting?

Keep a close eye on the rule changes when the fast track limit changes.

ATE is worthwhile, given the potentially expensive reports.

Please do not hesitate to contact me via my LinkedIn page for ATE recommendations.

Defendant

Insured?

Certificate of insurance?

Portal issues?

Can you value the claim at this stage?

Is the Defendant capable of satisfying a debt in a personal capacity?

Social media

Have you checked social media?

Ensure your client receives advice at the outset regarding Defendant investigations and fundamental dishonestly. Include in your terms and conditions and remind at the key stages.

Costs

Obviously dependent on case value, cost draftsmen still play an important role.

A positive, working relationship with a specialist draftsman is very important.

Draftsmen can assist with budgets and advice regarding portal/fixed costs issues.

CHAPTER NINE
PORTAL, DISCLOSURE
AND COSTS

Civil Liberties Bill

The 'Civil Liberties Bill' is scheduled for April 2020. It is possible this could be pushed back to October 2020. The small claims track for road traffic accident personal injury claims will increase to £5000 from £1000, and other personal injury claims will rise to £2000.

Current regime

The table below outlines a summary of the cost rules for processing claims in the "Low Value Portal", also pointing out the costs that are recoverable.

Public Liability and Highways Claims – Fixed Costs – Costs for Claims That Exit The Portal after 31 July 2013 – CPR 45

Fixed costs where a claim no longer continues under the EL/PL Protocol – <u>public liability claims</u>			
A. If Parties reach a settlement prior to the claimant issuing proceedings under Part 7			

Agreed damages	At least £1,000, but not more than £5,000	More than £5,000, but not more than £10,000	More than £10,000, but not more than £25,000
Fixed costs	The total of— (a) £950; and(b) 17.5% of the damages	The total of— (a) £1,855; and(b) 10.5% of damages over £5,000	The total of— (a) £2,370; and(b) 10% of damages over £10,000
B. If proceedings are issued under Part 7, but the case settles before trial			
Stage at which case is settled	On or after the date of issue, but prior to the date of allocation under Part 26	On or after the date of allocation under Part 26, but prior to the date of listing	On or after the date of listing but prior the date of trial
Fixed costs damages	The total of— (a) £2,450; and(b) 17.5% of the damages	The total of— (a) £3,065; and(b) 22.5% of the damages	The total of— (a) £3,790; and(b) 27.5% of the damages

C. If the claim is disposed of at trial			
Fixed costs	The total of— (a) £3,790;(b) 27.5% of the damages agreed or awarded; and(c) the relevant trial advocacy fee		

Which claims do the portals apply to?

Public liability claims up to £25,000 for an accident on or after July 31st 2013 the 'Pre-Action Protocol for Low Value Personal Injury Public Liability Claims' will be applicable. The same occurs for a disease claim, if the Defendant has not received a letter before July 31st 2013.

Public liability portal costs

CPR 45.16 sets out the relevant fees that are recoverable in the Low Value Portal:

(1) This Section applies to claims that have been or should have been started under Part 8 in accordance with Practice Direction 8B ('the Stage 3 Procedure').

(2) Where a party has not complied with the relevant Protocol rule 45.24 will apply.

'The relevant Protocol' means

(b) the Pre-action Protocol for Low Value Personal Injury Claims (Employers' Liability and Public Liability) Claims ('the EL/PL Protocol)

TABLE 6A

Fixed costs in relation to the EL/PL Protocol			
Where the value of the claim for damages is not more than £10,000	Where the value of the claim for damages is more than £10,000, but not more than £25,000		
Stage 1 fixed costs	£300	Stage 1 fixed costs	£300
Stage 2 fixed costs	£600	Stage 2 fixed costs	£1300
Stage 3- Type A fixed costs	£250	Stage 3- Type A fixed costs	£250
Stage 3- Type B fixed costs	£250	Stage 3- Type B fixed costs	£250
Stage 3- Type C fixed costs	£150	Stage 3- Type C fixed costs	£150

What about public liability portal disbursements?

CPR 45.19 sets out the relevant disbursements recoverable in the PL portal:

(1) The court:

(a) may allow a claim for a disbursement of a type mentioned in paragraphs (2) or (3); but

__(b) will not allow a claim for any other type of disbursement.__

(2) In a claim to which either the RTA Protocol or EL/PL Protocol applies, the disbursements referred to in paragraph (1) are:

__(a) the cost of obtaining –__

__(i) medical records;__

__(ii) a medical report or reports or non-medical expert reports as provided for in the relevant Protocol;__

(b) court fees as a result of Part 21 being applicable;

(c) court fees payable where proceedings are started as a result of a limitation period that is about to expire;

(d) court fees in respect of the Stage 3 Procedure; and

(e) any other disbursement that has arisen due to a particular feature of the dispute.

Counsel's Advice on Quantum/Liability

Additional advice on the value of the claim

45.23B
Where:

(a) the value of the claim for damages is more than £10,000;

(b) an additional advice has been obtained from a specialist solicitor or from counsel;

(c) that advice is reasonably required to value the claim,

the fixed costs may include an additional amount equivalent to the Stage 3 Type C fixed costs. **This is £150.**

It is therefore important to note:

a. Counsel's advice on liability/causation **will not be recoverable as a disbursement**, under normal circumstances.

b. It will be important to look early to other courses of funding if advice is required on LEI/ATE/BTE cover. An indemnity will be required

Fixed costs in relation to the EL/PL Protocol			
Where the value of the claim for damages is not more than £10,000		**Where the value of the claim for damages is more than £10,000, but not more than £25,000**	
Stage 1 fixed costs	£300	Stage 1 fixed costs	£300
Stage 2 fixed costs	£600	Stage 2 fixed costs	£1300
Stage 3 - Type A fixed costs	£250	Stage 3 - Type A fixed costs	£250
Stage 3 - Type B fixed costs	£250	Stage 3 - Type B fixed costs	£250
Stage 3 - Type C fixed costs	£150	Stage 3 - Type C fixed costs	£150

Cases that exit the portal

FROM PORTAL TO FIXED RECOVERABLE COSTS

From July 31st 2013 any case, with the exception of industrial diseases cases exiting any portal now goes into the Fixed Recoverable Costs scheme – outlined below.

Fixed recoverable costs for PL claims falling out of the PL portal

	Pre-issue £1,000 – £5,000	Pre-issue £5,001 – £10,000	Pre-issue £10,001 – £25,000	Issued – Post issue Pre-Allocation	Issued – Post allocation Pre-listing	Issued –Post listing Pre-trial	Trial – Advocacy Fee
	Case Settles before issue	Case Settles before issue	Case Settles before issue				
Public Liability							
Fixed Costs	£950+ 17.5% of Damages	£1,855+ 10% of Damages over £5k	£2,370+ 10% of Damages over £10k	£2,450+ 17.5% of Damages	£3,065 + 22.5% of Damages	£3,790 + 27.5% of Damages	£500 (to £3,000) £710 (£3-10,000) £1,070 (£10-15,000) £1,705 (£15,000+)
Escape	+ 20%	+ 20%	+ 20%	+ 20%	+ 20%	+ 20%	na

What disbursements are recoverable under fixed recoverable costs for PL claims?

45.29I sets out the relevant disbursements that are recoverable under FRCs for claims that start in the portal and then fall out:

(1) The court:

(a) may allow a claim for a disbursement of a type mentioned in paragraphs (2) or (3); but

(b) will not allow a claim for any other type of disbursement.

(2) In a claim started under either the RTA Protocol or the EL/PL Protocol, the disbursements referred to in paragraph (1) are:

(a) the cost of obtaining medical records and expert medical reports as provided for in the relevant Protocol;

(b) the cost of any non-medical expert reports as provided for in the relevant Protocol;

(c) the cost of any advice from a specialist solicitor or counsel as provided for in the relevant Protocol;

(d) court fees;

(e) any expert's fee for attending the trial where the court has given permission for the expert to attend;

(f) expenses which a party or witness has reasonably incurred in travelling to and from a hearing or in staying away from home for the purposes of attending a hearing;

(g) a sum not exceeding the amount specified in Practice Direction 45 for any loss of earnings or loss of leave by a party or witness due to attending a hearing or to staying away from home for the purpose of attending a hearing; and

(h) any other disbursement reasonably incurred due to a particular feature of the dispute.

Fixed costs – exit?

Under 45.29J, the Court can order an amount greater than fixed recoverable costs:

*(1) If it considers that there are **exceptional circumstances making it appropriate to do so**, the court will consider a claim for an amount of costs (excluding disbursements) which is greater than the fixed recoverable costs referred to in rules 45.29B to 45.29H.*

(2) If the court considers such a claim to be appropriate, it may:

(a) summarily assess the costs; or

(b) make an order for the costs to be subject to detailed assessment.

(3) If the court does not consider the claim to be appropriate, it will make an order:

(a) if the claim is made by the claimant, for the fixed recoverable costs; or

(b) if the claim is made by the defendant, for a sum which has regard to, but which does not exceed the fixed recoverable costs, and any permitted disbursements only.

However, standard highways and/or Public Liability cases are unlikely to be exceptional. It could be argued complex beauty / cosmetic claims are exceptional.

CPR 45.29k, sets out what happens if there is a failure to achieve an amount greater than fixed recoverable costs.

Failure to achieve costs greater than fixed recoverable costs

45.29K

(1) This rule applies where:

(a) costs are assessed in accordance with rule 45.29J(2); and

(b) the court assesses the costs (excluding any VAT) as being an amount which is in a sum less than 20% greater than the amount of the fixed recoverable costs.

(2) The court will make an order for the party who made the claim to be paid the lesser of:

(a) the fixed recoverable costs; and

(b) the assessed costs.

From April 2013 FA uplifts and ATE premiums were abolished, the result of this being that only the base fee can be re-claimed in a post-Jackson era. Although the introduction of 'Fixed Recoverable Costs' now might make these types of claims unappealing to take on, it is important to remember that the fees obtained for advancing to trial are still reasonable and do not vary significantly from the fees pre-Jackson.

https://www.justice.gov.uk/courts/procedure-rules/civil/protocol/pre-action-protocol-for-low-value-personal-injury-employers-liability-and-public-liability-claims

CHAPTER TEN
COSMETIC SURGERY

Introduction

Valued at around £3.6 billion in the UK, the cosmetic surgery industry is growing rapidly. The majority of clients have to opt for private procedures, due to the fact that cosmetic surgery is not very often made available on the NHS. Although some procedures are non-surgical, they still carry a various degree of risk such as laser hair removal, microdermabrasion and chemical peels, botox and dermal fillers, tattoo removal, skin lightening and permanent make up. However, understandably surgical procedures such as breast enlargements and reductions, facelifts, liposuction, tummy tucks, nose jobs, hair transplants and ear corrections carry a much more serious degree of risk. The NHS will only intervene if a complication to cosmetic surgery is life threatening and needs rectifying. Failure from your client to choose a registered and experienced surgeon could be detrimental.

Marketing and Advertising

The marketing and advertising of cosmetic surgery is a major contributing factor to its increasing popularity. Due to the fiercely competitive nature of the industry, social media is an ideal platform for cosmetic clinics to reach out to their desired target audience and they know how to use marketing techniques effectively. Aesthetically captivating emails and newsletters detailing offers sell procedures, allowing surgeons and clinics to benefit financially.

Hopefully before engaging in any type of cosmetic surgery your client will have carried out independent research. However, fabricated reviews from alleged 'highly satisfied' customers on social media can be misleading, meaning it's highly likely your client could have been manipulated by this. Clinics rely on repeat custom and positive recommendations.

The language used in advertising campaigns is another important element to consider. Generic terms such as the 'best surgeons', 'safe' and 'results' are words that frequent the material. Try and obtain copies if possible, to look for evidence of false or misleading advertising.

Offers

Guidance set by the General Medical Council suggests that promotional tactics should not be used to entice people to make a decision they may regret later. Clinics should not use the incentive of financial savings as a way of gaining custom, such as a '2 for 1' offer. Often the offers available have an expiry date, this is a dangerous tactic used in marketing because it is essentially rushing people to make a potentially life changing decision.

General Medical Council Guidelines

New guidelines set by the General Medical Council and placed into effect from June 1st 2016 outlined general rules that all doctors conducting cosmetic surgery should adhere to.

- **Consent** Before engaging in any type of procedure the patient needs to have given full consent.

- **Information** It is the responsibility of the doctor to educate the client about the procedure and to talk them through exactly what will happen, the potential risks involved and the aftercare that is available. Doctors should have thoroughly discussed their medical history and have taken next of kin details.

- **Marketing** must be done sensibly and should not in any way attempt to mislead clients. Financial savings should not be used as the main incentive for surgery and in no way should the marketing campaign underestimate the risks involved.

- **Assessment** Thorough assessment of the client should be carried out to establish that cosmetic surgery is the correct route for them and that psychologically they are well enough to proceed.

- **General** Patient safety and respect should always be at the forefront. Doctors should be upfront with patients about their capabilities and credentials and outline any concerns they have. They should always adhere to the appropriate rules and guidelines.

Choosing a Surgeon

The General Medical Council register lists around 245,000 doctors in the UK. The register guarantees that 'revalidation' checks have been carried out every five years to check the doctor is physically and mentally capable of doing their job. An appraisal is conducted annually and reviews from patients they have carried procedures out on are looked into. The GMC has the authority to restrict, temporarily suspend or completely remove the doctor from the register, which would end their career if they feel he or she is a danger to patients.

It should be noted that doctors who carry out private cosmetic surgery do not have to be listed as a specialist in the area, they only legally have to be registered to work as a doctor. Doctors from other countries often enter the UK to work in clinics and are not on the GMC register, if they aren't then it unfortunately means the patient does not have the guarantee they would with a fully registered professional.

Although not legally required, surgeons should be a member of 'BAPRAS' – British Association of Plastic Reconstructive and Aesthetic Surgeons, or 'BAAPS' The British Association of Aesthetic Plastic Surgeons.

Helpful guidance:

https://baaps.org.uk/patients/

Medical history and psychological assessment

Records

Before conducting a procedure, practitioners should refer to a patient's medical history and to try and establish exactly why they want the treatment. Due to the fact that the majority of cosmetic surgery is carried out in private establishments, there is no legal demand stating that medical records should be referred to.

Patients usually have to complete a form stating if they have any objections to their GP being contacted or not, a lot of patients do not want their GP to know they have undergone a procedure.

Psychology

The psychological state of a patient is also another important aspect that responsible practitioners should be keen to consider. The practitioner should have spent time consulting with the patient before the procedure. Alternative, less invasive options should have been discussed if a similar outcome could have been achieved with less risk. A patient considering surgery might be in a fragile state of mind and low self-esteem makes them highly vulnerable. Your client should have made the decision alone, without influence or pressure from the surgeon.

Body dysmorphic disorder is a mental disorder where a person is preoccupied with flaws, or imaginary flaws in their appearance, it is perhaps the most important condition for a practitioner to identify.

It is the duty of the practitioner to ensure your client was not pressured into a procedure and they should have actively encouraged them to spend time contemplating before committing. A consent form should also have been given to the patient clearly outlining details of how the work will be conducted, the potential side effects and risks involved and also the after-care package. Failure to do this may add further to the case against them.

Regulating cosmetic procedures

The regulation of cosmetic surgery is extremely challenging. If a Doctor is registered with the GMC then checks are carried out - the same goes for nurses, if fully registered they are regulated by the nursing and midwifery council. However, for those that are not registered, patients are putting themselves in an extremely vulnerable position and are potentially placing their lives in danger. Difficulty in regulating non-UK surgeons who enter the country to carry out a procedure is particularly difficult because their qualifications and level of expertise may well not be at the standard it should be.

The establishment should be fully registered with the 'CQC', Care Quality Commission – failure to register may well mean that the clinic is not practicing legally and following the correct guidelines, it also potentially voids insurance. It is a legal requirement to register with the CQC if invasive surgery is being carried out and instruments or equipment are being inserted, such as breast implants. Laser lipolysis and procedures involving the eye such as refractive eye, or lens implant surgery are also procedures that insist the clinic or hospital needs to be registered. Less invasive procedures such as laser hair removal, botox, dermal fillers and chemical peels are not regulated by the CQC.

Following the PIP implant scandal, The Department of Health's report, the 'Review of Regulation of Cosmetic Interventions' urged that medical practitioners should be fully qualified and that any non-surgical procedures should always be conducted under the authority of a professional who is competent and qualified to administer the treatment.

The review suggested that more legal requirements should be introduced, such as a code of conduct and a detailed register of every practitioner who performs a cosmetic procedure, either surgical or non-surgical. Dermal fillers should be listed as prescription only and in an attempt to combat the misleading marketing aspect, financial reductions on surgical procedures should be banned. The report also outlined the requirement for an ombudsman to represent the private healthcare sector and professional indemnity needs to be mandatory.

The Cosmetic Surgery (Minimum Standards Bill) 2012-2013 was introduced as a way of ensuring minimum standards would be met for all cosmetic procedures. The bill outlined new guidelines such as the introduction of the "United Kingdom Implant Registry", where manufacturing details about the implant, the clinic where the procedure was carried out and the patient who has received the treatment are stored on record. It will also be compulsory for anyone carrying out procedures to register with the "United Kingdom Cosmetic Surgery Regulatory and Standards Authority", more commonly known as 'OffCos', they will also regulate non-surgical procedures. The bill urges the importance of banning the advertising and marketing of cosmetic surgery.

The Royal College of Surgeons also intervened and introduced a certification scheme. The scheme was designed to assure patients before they undergo treatment that the surgeon they have selected is fully qualified and has experience carrying out the procedure successfully.

Common Procedures that claims are taken out against

As with any type of procedure, there is no guarantee that the results will be exactly as expected and often patients will feel dissatisfied with the treatment they have received. Choosing a recommended and registered surgeon/clinic alleviates the possibility of something going wrong, but in many cases patients feel they have a right to claim.

The most common procedures that claims are taken out against are botox and dermal fillers, breast enlargement or reductions, nose or ear reshaping, facelifts, liposuction, tummy tucks, gastric bands, facelifts, laser skin procedures and brow lifts. A patient may feel they are obliged to claim because the correct consent was not obtained, or if there have been unexpected complications after such as, nerve damage or damage to the organs or arteries. Cosmetic dentistry is another procedure where many claims are also made.

Limitation Act 1980

Under the 'Limitation Act 1980' any claims must be 'brought' within 3 years, from the date of the procedure.

Claims taken out against a surgeon or clinic will be carried out under tort law and it needs to be established if there have been any elements of medical negligence. A claim may be taken out against the company that have carried out the procedure (the company may dispute that the contract was taken out between the patient and the practitioner), or it may be taken out against the individual practitioner

Claiming against the individual surgeon may be problematic if the surgeon is not a UK resident, if they have not taken out the correct insurance policy, or if there is a debate regarding the employment status of the surgeon within the company.

Damages for pain, suffering, loss of amenity or special damages may be sought. Depending on the severity of the scars, burns or psychological damage, claims can range between hundreds to thousands of pounds. Photographic evidence is imperative.

CHAPTER ELEVEN
CHILDREN

Introduction

Manufacturers advise that hair dye products must not be used by children under the age of 16, due to the fact they contain dangerous chemicals that could cause an allergic reaction, sometimes even fatal. The European Commission has argued that this should be clearly stated on the packaging and the potential risks of using the product made clear.

However, despite being fully aware of the dangers of using hair dye on children, some salons choose to ignore this guidance and are therefore putting vulnerable children at serious risk. Research carried out by BBC Wales shockingly discovered that a 12-year-old girl was offered a hair colouring appointment at 16 different establishments! The undercover girl was only refused an appointment by 1 responsible salon and was turned away due to her age.

Patch Test

It is especially important for teenagers (over 16) and young people, that a patch test is carried out every single time a hair dye product is applied, even if it is a product regularly used. Patch tests should be carried out for both home hair dye kits and in salons. A small sample of the dye should be applied to the skin, behind the ear for example and left for 48 hours to check for any sign of a reaction. If there is no reaction then it is okay to proceed to use the product. However, if there is a subtle hint of any reaction to the hair dye then it must not be applied.

Salon owner, Donna Wallbank from Brynmawr, Blaenau Gwent has agreed with the importance of a patch test and admitted that more and more clients are showing signs of an allergic reaction.

User of a home hair dye kit, Sammi Ford was unfortunate enough to experience the downside of not carrying out a patch test on her home dye kit and suffered an extreme reaction. Initially her head began to burn and itch and the reaction progressed to such an extent that her eyes were swollen and painful sores appeared all over her face.

After witnessing the undercover experiment, Shirley Davis, the 'Hair Council's Welsh representative expressed her dismay at the fact a young child had willingly been offered a colouring appointment at 16 out of 17 salons. Davis commented, "Everyone within the industry is trying to professionalise it and we have salons that are actually contemplating colouring a young person's hair. If they did something with this young girl and she had an anaphylactic shock she could die – that's how serious it is. "You have to patch test over-16 and under 16 it's a no-no."

Regulation and insurance

The scale of hairdressing businesses ranges massively, some are mobile stylists who carry out treatments at home and others are successful franchises serving thousands of people. Lack of insurance is the main issue in placing a claim for hair damage.

Shockingly, as discussed earlier in this book, the hair dressing industry is not regulated, which means anyone can open a salon regardless of their training, qualifications and experience – due to this people's lives are being put at risk, especially when considering the dangerous chemicals that are used on a daily basis and the potentially fatal risk that having a severe allergic reaction carries.

The most important type of insurance for a business interacting with members of the public is public liability insurance, this covers them if an injury or accident was to occur and a claim was taken out against them. Legally it is not an obligation for hairdressers or beauticians to have public liability insurance, but due to the serious nature of the risks involved with some treatments or procedures it is recommended to have adequate insurance in case a client decides to sue.

Common hairdressing claims

- **Over-lapping** – Repeating a procedure too soon, or applying a treatment to hair that has recently undergone a similar process is a popular basis for claims. Inexperienced or unqualified hairdressers might apply a hair dye to hair that has been recently dyed, causing a likely risk of breakage.

- **Over processing** – This occurs when a product has been left on longer that it should have been, a large quantity of products has been used, or the concentration of the product was too high. A child has much thinner and more fragile hair than an adult, meaning they are more vulnerable and prone to breakage, potentially even damaging the hair permanently and risking alopecia later in life.

- **Allergic reaction** – The hairdresser must always perform a patch test 48 hours prior to the treatment. Children have highly sensitive skin and scalps, so the risk of them having a reaction is significantly higher, this is why manufacturers suggest a minimum age of 16.

- **Straightening** – The chemical straightening of hair is another popular, but potentially dangerous procedure and should not be over-lapped, as this can leave hair prone to breakage. Claims are often taken out against this treatment, especially if testing has not been completed beforehand. The treatment should not be carried out on children under any circumstance because it can cause hair to become damaged and in extreme cases, eventually snap off. There is also the added risk of an allergic reaction due to exposing them to the chemicals used.

- **Perms** – A lot of claims are taken out against hairdressers or salons who have provided a perming treatment. The chemicals used are highly dangerous and failure to carry out a patch test, or by applying an incorrect perming solution can result in burns and blistering to the scalp or permanent damage to the hair. This could have a devastating impact on a child's sensitive scalp. A fully qualified stylist should also be aware that perms are not suitable for every hair type and colour.

- **Extensions** – The increased popularity of hair extensions has seen a rise in claims against this procedure being taken out. Hairdressers who are not fully qualified to fit extensions often offer this treatment at an affordable price and many problems can arise. The first is if the extensions are a bad fit or if the wrong type, or quantity of bonds are used – causing headaches and hair damage. Hair extensions are a cause of alopecia and applying them to a child's hair can be highly dangerous because the fragility of their hair cannot hold the weight of extensions.

- Management and aftercare should also have been discussed in depth. Failure to educate the client extensively about this can result in pain and matted, permanently damaged hair. The removal of hair extensions requires a skilled professional, as hair can become damaged throughout this process and poor management may result in them having to be cut out to remove them properly. Successful claims are often strongly supported by a series of photos taken throughout the entire extension fitting and removing process.

But remember, children just shouldn't be undertaking any form of beauty treatment. If a salon carries out beauty treatment including hair dying and the treatment goes wrong liability should be admitted immediately. Remember to check your clients date of birth at the date the negligent treatment was carried out.

CHAPTER TWELVE
CONCLUSION

I hope this guide has provided you with a basic understanding of the most common beauty and cosmetic claims. Section 1 has hopefully offered a detailed insight into the beauty industry and the procedures where popular claims arise from. Negligence within the hairdressing industry, product liability and the campaign against PPD are also important elements to consider. The case studies were hopefully of interest.

A practical guide features in Section 2 with the aim of educating you further on how to run a successful claim. A detailed insight into claims regarding surgical procedures and also the dangers of hairdressing treatments on children has also been outlined.

Before accepting new instructions, it is always wise to undertake further reading and to start marketing initiatives on a small scale (an additional advert to your monthly newsletter, for example.)

The most valuable experience is always gained from actually running the cases and this type of work is extremely worthwhile for claimants who have identifiable injuries. Development of other areas can arise from having a specialist knowledge in beauty treatment such as, dermatitis and cosmetic surgery claims.

The Civil Liberties Bill, including the change to the small claims limit will undoubtedly affect the profitability of such claims. A comprehensive vetting process and a proactive claim management procedure will ensure this is a profitable area of work for a solicitor looking to transfer to a new practice area, away from road traffic claims. There will be a limit in terms of new instructions and therefore, quality is key.

MORE BOOKS BY
LAW BRIEF PUBLISHING

A selection of our other titles available now:-

'A Practical Guide to the SRA Principles, Individual and Law Firm Codes of Conduct 2019 – What Every Law Firm Needs to Know' by Paul Bennett
'A Practical Guide to Licensing Law for Commercial Property Lawyers' by Niall McCann & Richard Williams
'A Practical Guide to Adoption for Family Lawyers' by Graham Pegg
'Essential Motor Finance Law for the Busy Practitioner' by Richard Humphreys
'A Practical Guide to Industrial Disease Claims' by Andrew Mckie & Ian Skeate
'Employment Law and the Gig Economy' by Nigel Mackay & Annie Powell
'A Practical Guide to the Law of Armed Conflict' by Jo Morris & Libby Anderson
'A Practical Guide to Redundancy' by Philip Hyland
'A Practical Guide to Vicarious Liability' by Mariel Irvine
'A Practical Guide to Claims Arising from Delays in Diagnosing Cancer' by Bella Webb
'A Practical Guide to Applications for Landlord's Consent and Variation of Leases' by Mark Shelton
'A Practical Guide to Relief from Sanctions Post-Mitchell and Denton' by Peter Causton
'Butler's Equine Tax Planning: 2nd Edition' by Julie Butler
'A Practical Guide to Equity Release for Advisors' by Paul Sams
'A Practical Guide to Immigration Law and Tier 1 Entrepreneur Applications' by Sarah Pinder
'A Practical Guide to Unlawful Eviction and Harassment' by Stephanie Lovegrove
'In My Backyard! A Practical Guide to Neighbourhood Plans' by Dr Sue Chadwick
'A Practical Guide to the Law Relating to Food' by Ian Thomas

'A Practical Guide to Cosmetic Surgery Claims' by Dr Victoria Handley
'A Practical Guide to Chronic Pain Claims' by Pankaj Madan
'A Practical Guide to Claims Arising from Fatal Accidents' by James Patience
'A Practical Approach to Clinical Negligence Post-Jackson' by Geoffrey Simpson-Scott
'A Practical Guide to Personal Injury Trusts' by Alan Robinson
'Employers' Liability Claims: A Practical Guide Post-Jackson' by Andrew Mckie
'A Practical Guide to Subtle Brain Injury Claims' by Pankaj Madan
'The Law of Driverless Cars: An Introduction' by Alex Glassbrook
'A Practical Guide to Costs in Personal Injury Cases' by Matthew Hoe
'A Practical Guide to Alternative Dispute Resolution in Personal Injury Claims – Getting the Most Out of ADR Post-Jackson' by Peter Causton, Nichola Evans, James Arrowsmith
'A Practical Guide to Personal Injuries in Sport' by Adam Walker & Patricia Leonard
'The No Nonsense Solicitors' Practice: A Guide To Running Your Firm' by Bettina Brueggemann
'Baby Steps: A Guide to Maternity Leave and Maternity Pay' by Leah Waller
'The Queen's Counsel Lawyer's Omnibus: 20 Years of Cartoons from The Times 1993-2013' by Alex Steuart Williams

These books and more are available to order online direct from the publisher at www.lawbriefpublishing.com, where you can also read free sample chapters. For any queries, contact us on 0844 587 2383 or mail@lawbriefpublishing.com.

Our books are also usually in stock at www.amazon.co.uk with free next day delivery for Prime members, and at good legal bookshops such as Hammicks and Wildy & Sons.

We are regularly launching new books in our series of practical day-to-day practitioners' guides. Visit our website and join our free newsletter to be kept informed and to receive special offers, free chapters, etc.

You can also follow us on Twitter at www.twitter.com/lawbriefpub.